Correct Me If I'm WRONG

collected by the **Columbia Journalism Review**
edited by **Gloria Cooper**

published by

NEWSEUM

Errare humanum est.

Poll says that 53% believe media offen make mistakes

The San Diego Union-Tribune 07/12/98

Plan to deny welfare to immigrants still alive

The Grand Rapids (Mich.) *Press* 01/15/95

School testing mushrooms

Marshfield (Wis.) *News-Herald* 08/25/98

Boy, declared dead, revives as family protests

The Columbus (Ohio) *Dispatch* 09/29/91

Base closings get Bush's OK; Congress next

The Indianapolis Star 09/16/05

Editor's wife rented to 2 suspects, FBI says

Chicago Tribune 10/15/01

Trial ends in mercy killing

The Burlington (Vt.) *Free Press* 12/01/88

Head lice are for everyone, experts say

The Daily News, Middlesboro, Ky. 09/19/91

Asteroid Nearly Misses Earth

The Washington Post 06/24/02

Man shot in back, head found in street

Daily Globe, Worthington, Minn. 12/08/84

Westinghouse Gives Robot Rights to Firm

The Washington Post 06/12/87

Crowds Rushing To See Pope Trample 6 To Death

Journal Star, Peoria, Ill. 07/09/80

For some context, consider these numbers from the same year, as reported by the Cleveland Plain Dealer: 91 percent of clergy were men, 92 percent of engineers were men, 90 percent of men were dentists.

York (Pa.) *Daily Record* 04/24/97

After his speech, the governor, accompanied by six children, his entourage and dozens of reporters, climbed out of his pool to pace along his chain-link fence, occasionally standing on his hind legs and tilting his head back.

Los Angeles Times 02/28/96

Bill to halt illness passes

The Sun, Baltimore 04/04/00

Collene Campbell champions the rights of murder victims after being one herself more than once

The Orange County Register, Santa Ana, Calif. 09/30/01

Candlelight ceremony unties couple

The Morris (Ill.) *Daily Herald* 09/16/81

Japanese scientists grow frog eyes and ears

Daily Camera, Boulder, Colo. 01/04/00

Marijuana issue sent to a joint committee

The Toronto Star 06/14/96

Sexual misconduct alleged at city hall

PICTURE Bruce Edwards

The Edmonton Journal, Canada 09/24/86

British foot-in-mouth remedy: massive slaughter

The Gazette, Colorado Springs, Colo. 03/16/01

Principal transfers upset parents

The Des Moines (Iowa) *Register* 05/12/01

Bush argues that economy is 'fundamentally string'

The Boston Globe Online 07/16/02

“After finding no qualified candidates for the position of principal, the school department is extremely pleased to announce the appointment of David Steele to the post,” said Philip Streifer, Superintendent of Schools. “David was the best choice.”

Barrington (R.I.) *Times* 03/06/91

Oozing corpses raising eyebrows

San Francisco Chronicle 05/27/05

Dog judging course offered at college

The Indiana (Pa.) *Gazette* 07/05/89

Take pride; don't lose site of why you teach

A message from state's 'Teacher of the Year'

The Voice for Education, Harrisburg, Pa. 02/89

Armin Shimerman (shown here without makeup) is back as Quark in the new 'Star Trek: Deep Space Nine.'

The News & Observer, Raleigh, N.C. 01/04/93

U.S. advice: Keep drinking water from sewage

Journal and Courier, Lafayette, Ind. 09/17/92

Babies are what the mother eats

The Times-Herald, Newport News, Va. 07/11/84

Panda Lectures This Week at National Zoo

The Washington Post 01/13/01

Dr. Tackett Gives Talk On Moon

Indiana (Pa.) *Evening Gazette* 03/13/76

Dishonesty policy voted in by Senate

Ball State Daily News, Muncie, Ind. 02/08/85

Despite our best efforts, black employment is still rising

The Evening Times, West Palm Beach, Fla. 10/03/80

Steamed pudding and crap dip

The Sacramento (Calif.) *Bee* 12/27/98

After Spill, Jockey's Business Falls Off

The Washington Post 12/04/87

Starving Angolans eating dogs, bark

The Pretoria News, South Africa 09/10/94

Get tough seat belt policy working

The Courier News, Bridgewater, N.J. 01/24/96

Red Tape Holds Up New Bridge

Milford (Conn.) *Citizen* 07/12/82

Flier to duplicate Miss Earhart's fatal flight

The New Jersey Herald, Newton 01/09/84

Defendant's speech ends in long sentence

Minneapolis Tribune 02/25/81

Ford, Reagan Neck in Presidential Primary

Ethiopian Herald 02/24/76

Solar system expected to be back in operation

Libertyville (Ill.) *Herald* 03/15/78

Attorneys refusing to represent indignant suspects in WNC

Asheville (N.C.) *Citizen-Times* 04/15/01

NRC: Fuel rods mistakenly stored in safe place

The Greenwich (Conn.) *Time* 1/16/02

Jeanette Lindholm Receives Doctorette

The Independent, Ortonville, Minn. 05/27/92

Hitler used to sell potato chips

The New Mexican, Santa Fe 06/02/98

Whether it's traditional roses and tulips or a cluster of more exotic blooms, the bouquet adds a fresh finishing touch to the bride's ensemble. Her gown, above, is from the After Sex Bridal Collection.

The Berkshire Eagle, Pittsfield, Mass. 01/28/90

CORRECTION/CLARIFICATION

The Region. A photo caption in Wednesday's editions about a newborn gorilla at the Pittsburgh Zoo incorrectly identified a male gorilla in the picture. It was the brother of the infant, not the father.

Pittsburgh Post-Gazette 08/09/96

Rancho Bernardo's only full-sized community newspaper!
Disturbing to over 18,000 households per week!

Spirit of the Fourth, Rancho Bernardo, Calif. 07/04/89

Tobacco ads dishonest, too small, Sullivan says

New Haven (Conn.) *Register* 06/12/90

Carol Hendrix of York produces about 960 eggs per year, more than three times that of the average chicken.

York (Pa.) *Daily Record* 04/13/90

N.C. State cattle researchers look over a Jersey cow, that was impregnated with semen donated by a Maine dairy farmer.

Wilmington (N.C.) *Morning Star* 08/08/95

'Women in Politics' workshop postponed; make-up not set

The Charlotte (N.C.) *Observer* 11/13/91

First bike rally ends with five deaths; No major problems

The State, Columbia, S.C. 05/23/05

Jeffco limits sex offenders to one per home

The Denver Post 01/25/00

Chinese diver wins one-metre event; mates on carpet

The Toronto Star 01/11/98

Nuns forgive break-in, assault suspect

The Columbus (Ohio) *Dispatch* 07/15/98

Water parasite fears move to Alberta

The Province, Alberta, Canada 05/06/01

Police oversight group likes San Jose model

Austin (Texas) *American-Statesman* 12/21/99

Finally, we have made the commitment to our readers to minimize "jumps," those stories that continue from one page to another. Readers have told newspapers loud and often that they do not like such "jumps," and we've resolved to arrange our pages so that most stories will finish on the page they began.

See CHANGE/ Page A-2

Star-News, Pasadena, Calif. 01/28/92

Correction

Erroneous information was inadvertently inserted into the biographical summary accompanying a story on Peter Keefe in Tuesday's *Democrat and Chronicle*. Keefe cannot simultaneously whistle, stand on his head and drink beer.

Democrat and Chronicle, Rochester, N.Y. 10/17/93

Dad's sudden death vexes his family

The Oakland (Calif.) *Tribune* 07/02/96

Nude pub lawyer promises neighborly approach

The Review, Clackamas County, Ore. 04/13/89

Barbara of Seville' Opens Valley Opera Season

The Independent, Livermore, Calif. 10/27/99

HAIR REGROWTH LINIMENT

TEl: 7712874, 7711632

FAX: 5138943

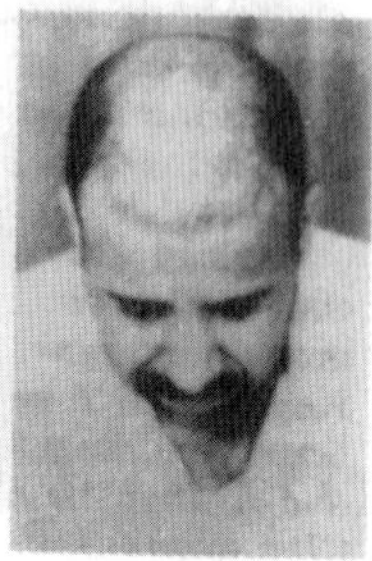

After

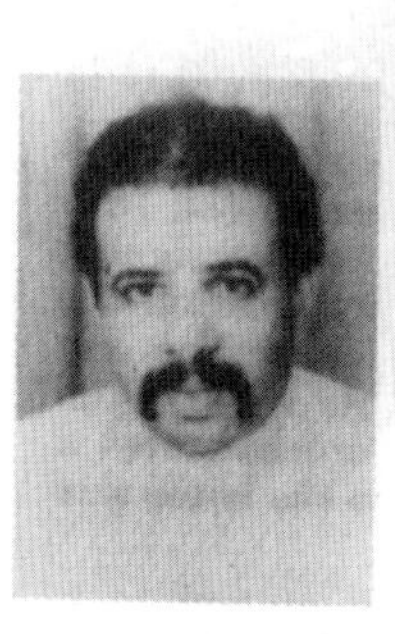

Before

China Daily 09/25/90

Death toll in India still rising

Relatives in Wilson heartened by news

The Wilson (N.C.) *Daily Times* 01/29/01

Actor's death during filming usually career-limiting move

The Toronto Star 04/21/93

Hillary Clinton on Welfare

Los Angeles Times 03/22/95

The earthquake that hit the Bay Area last Tuesday has caused a record 11-day layoff between Series games.

The earthquake also caused death and destruction.

The Honolulu Advertiser 10/24/89

Crack in toilet bowl leads to 3 arrests

The Pantagraph, Bloomington, Ill. 06/11/98

Dog chews on recall list

The Fresno (Calif.) *Bee* 12/31/99

Rumsfeld's pubic role is shrinking

The Providence (R.I.) *Journal* 08/08/04

Women compromise 26 percent of town's workers

Westport (Conn.) *News* 09/20/95

An item in Thursday's Nation Digest about the Massachusetts budget crisis made reference to new taxes that will help put Massachusetts "back in the African-American." The item should have said "back in the black."

The Fresno (Calif.) *Bee* 07/21/90

Empty Seat at Dinner Signals Turkey's Sensitivity Over Role

The New York Times 12/11/96

The Reverend Harry Phillips of Atlanta sodomized the 5:30 p.m. rites.

The Belton (S.C.) *News* 07/19/89

Police Stop Slaying Suspect Look-alikes

Yakima (Calif.) *Herald-Republic* 08/26/01

CORRECTION

■ The Jumble puzzle, which appeared on page D1 of Thursday's edition, actually was the puzzle scheduled to appear today. The Jumble originally scheduled to appear Thursday as well as the answers to Wednesday's puzzle are on page E1 today. The answers to the puzzle published today appeared Thursday, and the answers to the puzzle published Thursday will appear Saturday.

The Arizona Republic, Phoenix 09/28/84

Featured Services:

- Find a Loan
- Meet Someone
- Find a Hotel

MercuryNews.com, San Jose, Calif. 06/09/03

Obesity rubs off, study finds

The Cincinnati Post 10/15/03

Statistics on women
Some good and some bad

Women in Communications 02/76

Fried chicken cooked
in microwave wins trip

The Oregonian, Portland 07/08/81

**Rosemary Hall
Gets New Head**

The Hartford (Conn.) *Courant* 06/06/75

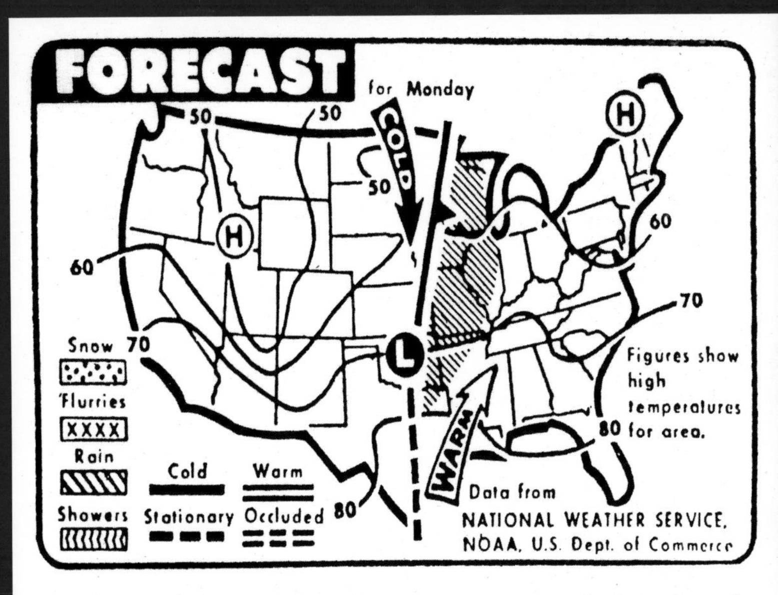

Shaded parts of map locate areas occupied by Israel since 1967.

Milwaukee Sentinel 10/31/77

Marion freed after 81-day ordeal

Ottawa Journal 10/28/77

82-day ordeal over

The Citizen, Ottawa 10/28/77

After 83 days, Marion safe

Ottawa Today 10/28/77

Correction

The band Raging Saint base their music on born-again Christian principles. They are not "unrepentant headbangers," as reported in the Night life column last Friday.

Austin (Texas) *American-Statesman* 03/10/87

Food stamp recipients turn to plastic

The Miami Herald 12/22/91

State Governments Are Sold on EBay for Surplus Auctions

San Francisco Chronicle 04/24/00

Actor sent to jail for not finishing sentence

News-Sentinel, Knoxville, Tenn. 01/21/89

A jury awarded the family $1.5 million in compensatory damages and $10 million in punitive damages. After deducting attorneys' fees and expenses, the family received $4.96 in punitive damages, with the father receiving half and the children splitting the difference.

The Kansas City (Mo.) *Star* 12/11/96

Chief Blue, the last full-blooded Catawba Indian Chief died in 1959. The Evening Herald incorrectly said Wednesday that he died three years ago due to a reporting error.

Evening Herald, Rock Hill, S.C. 09/02/76

Literarcy week observed

Messenger, Brandenburg, Ky. 09/04/85

Dead Expected To Rise

The Macon (Ga.) *News* 08/11/76

Indian Ocean talks

The Plain Dealer, Cleveland 10/05/77

EDITORS' NOTE: A mistake made by a transcription service mangled a quotation from William Bennett in Michael Kelly's July 17th Letter from Washington. In criticizing the political views of Patrick Buchanan, Mr. Bennett said "it's a real us-and-them kind of thing," not, as we reported, "it's a real S & M kind of thing."

The New Yorker 08/14/95

Beheading can cause kids stress

The Lompoc (Calif.) *Record* 07/26/95

He Found God At End of His Rope

Fort Worth (Texas) *Tribune* 02/03/78

Correction

It was incorrectly reported last Friday that today is T-shirt Appreciation Day. In fact, it is actually Teacher Appreciation Day.

Daily Vidette, Normal, Ill. 04/19/95

Older Americans Act Renewed

Not Born Yesterday!, La Canada, Calif. 01/01

Former Rep. Gray said last night: "Nobody's investigating me. Nobody's called me. I never had anything to do with selecting an architect. How can you investigate somebody for something he's never done? I've never received a nickel or any kind of favor from anybody associated with the building industry or an architectural firm in my 20 years in Congress."

Former Rep. Gray could not be reached for comment.

The Washington Post 11/11/76

2 producers quit show complaining report has more substance than hype

Naples (Fla.) *Daily News* 02/24/89

N.J. jails for women in need of a face lift

Daily Record, Morristown, N.J. 11/24/89

Find out how to handle complaints, and who can help your complaints fall on deaf ears.

The News Tribune, Woodbridge, N.J. 04/24/90

The degenerative manifestations of "old age" have included memory loss, disorientation, confusion, perceptional difficulties, speech loss, disorientation, confusion, perceptional difficulties, speech problems.

The Richmond (Ky.) *Register* 03/17/81

Robber Holds Up Albert's Hosiery

Buffalo (N.Y.) *Evening News* 09/19/75

Astronauts practice landing on laptops

The News-Press, Fort Myers, Fla. 03/13/94

Canadian seals deal with creditors

The Globe and Mail, Toronto 07/01/97

Condom faults could lead to dating policy

The Courier-News, Bridgewater, N.J. 06/15/88

Panel Urges Cloning Ethics Boards

Science 01/03/97

Salad still good after 50 years

Tribune-Star, Terre Haute, Ind. 03/11/98

More of us will live to be centurions

The Times Reporter, Dover-New Philadelphia, Ohio 02/11/87

462C UNIPRESSERS:

TO ALL OF YOU AND YOUR FAMILIES, MAY THIS BE A MOST PLEASANT HOLIDAY AND MAY THE NEW YEAR BE BRIGHT AND PROSPEROUS.

UPI 12-25 02:09 PPS

EDITORS: PLEASE DISREGARD 462C UNIPRESSERS. IT WAS INADVERTENTLY TRANSMITTED ON THIS CIRCUIT.

UPI 12-25 02:21 PPS

United Press International 12/25/74

➤ **Correction**: A story on Sally Ann Carey Thursday incorrectly stated that the family of a missing girl came to her for a psychic consultation. Two friends of the girl came to that session, and later Carey talked with the girl's mother. Also, Carey worked for Rutland Mental Health, not the Rutland Regional Medical Center. She taught swimming, not singing, adopted one child, not two, and at times contacts healing guides, not healing gods.

Rutland (Vt.) *Daily Herald* 12/17/94

SECRET CHURCH TRIAL FOR SEX-CHARGED PRIEST

Chicago Sun-Times 05/21/04

The President said the material he was making available should end, once and for all, speculation about his role in Watergate. mmmmmmmmmm

The Standard-Times, New Bedford, Mass. 04/30/74

Peace council to protest torture at radio station

The Post-Standard, Syracuse, N.Y. 01/11/08

Ralph Steiner Dead; A Still Photographer

The New York Times 07/15/86

U.S. offers 131-page guide to foreign terrorist groups

San Jose (Calif.) *Mercury News* 01/11/89

Recent visitors were Eli E. Millers and their son-in-law Jacob Hertzlers from Conewango, N.Y. settlement. Jacob had his tonsils removed in Hanover. It was a pleasant surprise to have them for supper.

The Budget, Sugar Creek, Ohio 03/02/90

The program on July 22 features a Southwest menu that includes a corn and black bean salad followed by a concert entitled "Wind Spectacular."

The New York Times 07/10/91

The house belongs to Emily Kesecker who is in a nursing home and has been boarded up for several years.

The Morgan Messenger, Berkeley Springs, W.Va. 02/03/93

Parking lot floods when man bursts

The Herald-Sun, Durham, N.C. 02/04/94

Cause of odor in Chester has been found: Henthorne

Panhandle Press, Chester, W.Va. 01/21/90

Parents object to human sacrifice school show

Pittsburgh Post-Gazette Online 12/19/02

EPA catalogs polluted rivers, one in Arkansas

Arkansas Gazette, Little Rock 06/15/89

A news analysis article on Saturday about the politics behind Gov. Pete Wilson's role in eliminating affirmative-action programs at University of California campuses rendered a word incorrectly in a quotation from Sherry Bebitch Jeffe, a former legislative aide in Sacramento. Ms. Jeffe said of Mr. Wilson: "He's been biding his time on this, knowing all along what he was going to do when the time was ripe. It's ripe. He's picked." She did not say, "He's pickled."

The New York Times 07/24/95

Never Withhold Herpes Infection From Loved One

Albuquerque (N.M.) *Journal* 12/26/84

Warranty aids home owners with defects

Knoxville (Tenn.) *News-Sentinel* 03/18/80

Youths steal funds for charity

The Reporter Dispatch, White Plains, N.Y. 02/17/82

Drunk gets nine months in violin case

The Lethbridge Herald, Canada 10/30/76

He also said an older woman suffered a broken hip when a dog pounced on her and read a long letter from someone supporting the dog ban.

The Tybee News, Tybee Island, Ga. 11/99

Alternative to jail is working in Albany

The Daily Gazette, Schenectady, N.Y. 02/06/98

"I think we are having some communications problems," Vogel said. "We are gon tg ivogeiSHRD

The Washington Post 06/24/79

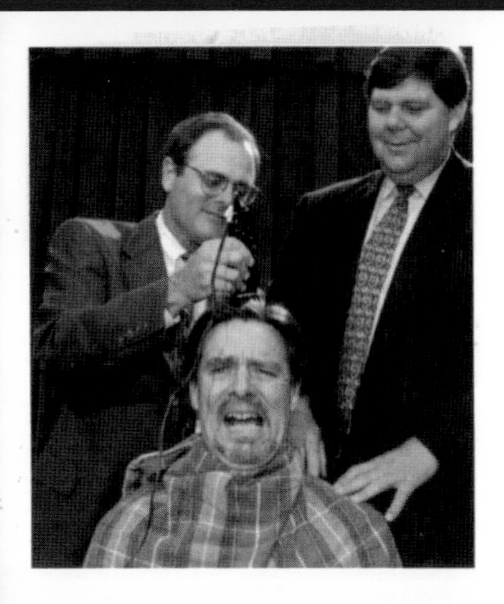

Programs to thwart elder abuse announced

Los Angeles Daily News 07/16/99

First female Marines train for combat with men

The Newton (Iowa) *Daily News* 04/01/97

High schoolers ignorant of finances, quiz shows

The Denver Post 05/23/97

Officials' heads to be displayed in lobby

The Daily Commercial, Leesburg, Fla. 09/09/03

X-ray of girl shows bureaucratic mentality

Globe and Mail, Toronto 01/18/88

Police jail nurse shot to death while driving home on freeway

Antelope Valley Press, Palmdale, Calif. 10/21/97

□

Journalists say voters hold key to November election

The Daytona Beach (Fla.) *News-Journal* 09/13/00

□

Weather

Sunny with a few cloudy periods today and Thursday, which will be followed by Friday. Details on Page 5.

The Province, Vancouver, Canada 06/21/78

Navy changes skirt policy, making apparel optional

The San Diego Union-Tribune 10/18/04

□

Sears to add 30 appliance outlets

Chicago Tribune 06/24/04

KELLY— Marie A. (nee Nissen), age 76, of Weehawken. Beloved mother of Kathleen and Kevin Kelly. Widow of the late Edward J. Kelly. Long-suffering Tenant of Gertrude Zeichner.

The Hudson Dispatch, Union City, N.J. 07/11/89

Last week for faulty art display

Central Florida Future, Orlando 10/04/00

Putin Cancels Plans for Trip After Bombing at Rock Concert

The New York Times 07/07/03

Blind woman forced by cop to clean up after her guide dog accepts settlement

Evening Times-Globe, Saint John, Canada 08/17/88

Hafen is an enthusiastic reader and claims "Lame is Rob" by Victor Hugo as her favorite book.

The Scroll (Rexburg, Idaho) 04/22/90

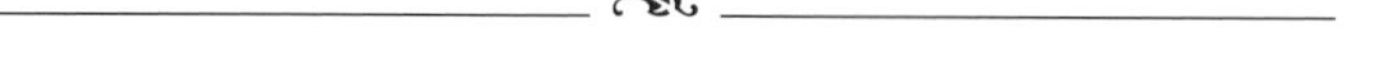

Woman Found Dead in Trunk Kept to Herself, Neighbors Say

The New York Times 10/28/02

Microsoft accuses federal judge of being impartial

The Appeal-Democrat, Marysville, Calif. 11/28/00

Correction

In last week's issue of Community Life, a picture caption listed some unusual gourmet dishes that were enjoyed at a Westwood Library party for students enrolled in a tutorial program for conversational English. Mai Thai Finn is one of the students in the program and was in the center of the photo. We incorrectly listed her name as one of the items on the menu. Community Life regrets the error.

Pascack Valley Community Life, Westwood, N.J. 02/25/81

ISU revokes doctorate in plagiarism

The Des Moines (Iowa) *Register* 12/14/95

$3 Million Verdict To Injured Detective Cut Nearly in Half

New York Law Journal 11/25/87

Genetically modified crops talk of meeting

The News Gazette,
Champaign, Ill. 01/21/01

Tools may be left inside patients during surgery

The Daily Orange, Syracuse, N.Y. 01/21/03

Some adults grow into blemishes

The Olympian, Olympia, Wash. 07/09/05

Tracy's Massage Receives License; Mayor Makes Yearly Appointments

Sioux Valley News, Canton, S.D. 05/05/94

Deer Kill 130,000

The Minneapolis Tribune 12/07/67

But let's look at the house again from the front, where the entrance foyer is flanked by a formal living room and dining room. Double closets in the foyer provide plenty of space to hang your coats and guests.

The Herald-Sun, Durham, N.C. 09/09/00

Farmer
Bill Dies
In House

The Atlanta Constitution 04/13/78

Corrections:

■ An April 5 story stated that Mary Fraijo did not return a reporter's calls seeking comment. Fraijo died last December.

The Spokesman-Review, Spokane, Wash. 04/11/96

Ballet lands Cuban dancers

2 recent defectors get contracts, 3rd gets shot

The Cincinnati Enquirer 02/19/04

Woman Saves Abenaki Tongue In Dictionary

The Times Argus, Barre-Montpelier, Vt. 05/02/94

Adults think teens having more sex than they are

Tonawanda (N.Y.) *News* 06/07/94

Tips to help prevent headaches after you die

The Record, Hackensack, N.J. 01/22/04

Sisters reunited after 18 years in checkout line at supermarket

Arkansas Democrat, Little Rock 09/29/83

Johnson Teacher Talks Very Slow

Indianapolis News 08/09/82

Setting the Record Straight

Last Sunday, The Herald erroneously reported that original Dolphin Johnny Holmes had been an insurance salesman in Raleigh, N.C., that he had won the New York lottery in 1982 and lost the money in a land swindle, that he had been charged with vehicular homicide but acquitted because his mother said she drove the car, and that he stated that the funniest thing he ever saw was Flipper spouting water on George Wilson. Each of these items was erroneous material published inadvertently. He was not an insurance salesman in Raleigh, did not win the lottery, neither he nor his mother was charged or involved in any way with a vehicular homicide, and he made no comment about Flipper or George Wilson. The Herald regrets the errors.

The Miami Herald 12/23/86

Newspaper have lots to worry about

Wisconsin State Journal, Madison 04/17/96

ABOUT COLUMBIA JOURNALISM REVIEW

Columbia Journalism Review's mission is to encourage and stimulate excellence in journalism in the service of a free society. It is both a watchdog and a friend of the press in all its forms, from newspapers to magazines to radio, television and the Web. Founded in 1961 under the auspices of Columbia University's Graduate School of Journalism, *CJR* examines day-to-day press performance as well as the forces that affect that performance. The magazine is published six times a year, and offers a deliberative mix of reporting, analysis, criticism and commentary. From the start, its most popular feature has been "The Lower Case," from which the items in this collection are drawn. CJR.org delivers real-time criticism and reporting, giving *CJR* a vital presence in the ongoing conversation about the media.

Gloria Cooper, the former deputy executive editor of *CJR*, edited its "Lower Case" page for more than three decades.

ABOUT THE NEWSEUM

The Newseum, located on historic Pennsylvania Avenue in Washington, D.C., blends five centuries of news history with up-to-the-second technology and hands-on interactive exhibits. The 250,000-square foot museum takes visitors behind the scenes of news and instills an appreciation of the importance of a free press and the First Amendment.

The Freedom Forum, a nonpartisan foundation dedicated to free press, free speech and free spirit, is the main funder of the Newseum's operations. The Newseum, while independent of any media companies, receives additional support from foundations, media organizations and individuals.

Correct Me If I'm Wrong: Press Bloopers As Seen in the Newseum,
Collected by Columbia Journalism Review

Newseum, 555 Pennsylvania Ave., N.W.,
Washington, DC 20001

Joe Urschel, executive director and senior vice president
Christy Mumford Jerding, editorial director
Kathy Terry, senior designer
Ann Marie Watson, publications editor
Paola Zamora, advertising designer

Design by Simmons Design, Alexandria, Va.

ISBN: 978-0-9799521-4-2

NEWSEUM

329.09-NEWS I 1/10 I 5k I BL